I MET A WOOLLY MAMMOTH

I MET A WOOLLY MAMMOTH
and other poems for kids

JOHN MARK GREEN

illustrated by Aya Suarjaya

DEDICATION

In memory of my mother Barbara who
sparked my love of reading and poetry.

A NOTE FROM THE AUTHOR

Though these poems are rather silly, they celebrate the joys of language, rhyme, and the wonderful world in which we live. I hope they will be read aloud by parents, teachers, and children of all ages.

CONTENTS

I MET A WOOLLY MAMMOTH

I met a woolly mammoth,
more shaggy than a sheep.
It stepped out of a science book,
then stumbled down my street.

Its tusks were long and curving,
its legs like hairy trees.
A long-haired, ragged elephant
was how it looked to me.

I thought it must be thirsty,
its fur coat looked so hot.
And when I got the garden hose
it really drank a lot!

That mammoth asked politely
(as nice as nice could be)
to step inside my house and have
a big bowl of ice cream.

MILLY O'MALLEY

Milly O'Malley from Kalamazoo
has a collection of horrible shoes.

Shoes that look ugly,
shoes that feel bad.
Shoes guaranteed
to make everyone mad.

Shoes that will trip you,
shoes that will pinch.
Shoes that refuse
to move even one inch.

It won't surprise you
to hear me say
that Milly O'Malley
goes barefoot all day.

HAIRY SPIDERS

I don't like hairy spiders
or their black, beady eyes.
To meet a hairy spider
is not a nice surprise.

Climbing on my ceiling,
high above my bed,
catching flies for dinner
within their sticky webs.

I think they're kind of creepy,
I wish they'd stay away.
A hairy, scary spider
would really wreck my day.

But I don't have to be afraid,
I'm larger, as you see.
Perhaps those tiny spiders
are scared of giant ME!

SILLY PICKLES

There are pickles in the pantry,
pickles everywhere!
Bouncing on the sofa
and sliding down the stairs.

Pickles on the rooftop,
pickles by the pool.
They're even in the freezer,
so cold they're turning blue.

Pickles in the bathtub,
something's really wrong.
Why aren't these silly pickles
in jars where they belong?

BEN'S NOISY NOSE

Ben had a nose that was noisy.
His sneeze shook windows and doors.
Whenever he blew, it honked like a goose,
and a trumpet-like sound came forth.

His nose never made him embarrassed.
"It's a jolly good sniffer," he'd say.
"Even though it is loud, it smells rather well.
I'd be sad if my snoot went away."

TINY DINO

I think a tiny dinosaur
would be the perfect pet,
to ride inside my backpack
and sleep under my bed.

I'd feed it and I'd walk it,
clean up its dino poo.
My friends would be so jealous,
they all would want one too.

A tiny dinosaur would be
the best gift I could get.
This Christmas would be perfect.
Please Santa, don't forget.

VEGGIE MAGIC

"Finish your veggies
if you want dessert."
So I slip some spinach
inside of my shirt.

I put peas in my pockets,
squash in my socks.
My dog wants the rest,
she's licking her chops.

Then, like a magician,
waving my wand...
"Can I have some cake?
My dinner's all gone!"

YAK IN A YURT

I know a yak
who lives in a yurt
and loves to eat yams
every day for dessert.

Also, for breakfast,
for lunch, and for tea.
He thinks that yams
are the best food to eat.

Yams on his table.
Yams in his hall.
Yams in the doorway,
when I come to call.

That yak loves to tell
of the yams on his shelf.
I wish that he'd yammer
about something else.

OOPS

When dressing for school,
I made a mistake.
A quite silly slip-up
that's easy to make.

I was in such a hurry
and trying to rush,
not wanting to miss
my ride on the bus.

What I didn't discover
until I'd arrived...
was that I'd worn my undies
on the outside!

HOME SWEET HOME

Snails don't stay in motels,
or camp outdoors in tents.
When they go on vacation,
it doesn't cost a cent.

Snails are quite content, you see,
to never leave their home.
Instead, they take it with them
wherever they may roam.

MOLLY MACAROON

Miss Molly Macaroon
played a brass bassoon,
at night in her yard
by the light of the moon.

She loved to play loudly,
though quite out of tune.
So dreadful was the sound
of her big brass bassoon.

Her neighbors lay sleepless,
they covered their heads,
hoping Molly would tire
and soon go to bed.

ANIMALS IN MY DREAMS

There's a weasel with an easel
painting pictures by the sea,
and an emu in a tutu
dancing ballet in the street.

There's a lion in a limo
driving all around the town,
and a badger baking brownies
in a bunker underground.

There's a spider on a tightrope
walking high above the crowd,
as a silverback gorilla
plays his trumpet way too loud.

There's a dodo selling donuts
on a dock in Timbuktu,
and a friendly, furry ferret
fishing from a blue canoe.

There's a wombat in a top hat
playing bagpipes in the sun,
and a marmot in a muumuu
going for her morning run.

There's a jaguar in a fast car
jousting with a jolly knight,
and an angry, orange ostrich
who forgot to be polite.

There's an ocelot in armor
eating marmalade and cheese.
Oh, they really are so silly,
all these animals in my dreams.

STINKY BIGFOOT

I bumped into a Bigfoot
while walking in the woods,
he burst out of the bushes
and stomped to where I stood.

He looked like a gorilla,
smelled like a garbage can,
his hair was brown and shaggy
and his breath was truly bad.

That Bigfoot sniffed me up and down,
then ran into the trees.
I think that he was frightened
because I smelled so clean.

WISHING FOR WINGS

I wish I had wings,
like those of a bird.
I wish I had wings,
though that might sound absurd.

I wish I had wings,
it would be so cool.
No more riding the bus,
I would just
        fly
           to
              school.

MY PET

I tried to take my pet to school,
and stirred up such a fuss.
The cranky driver wouldn't let
my pet get on the bus.

We walked instead, my teacher said,
"That can't be here with us!"
And all because my dear pet was
a hippopotamus.

HOMEWORK

I don't like doing homework,
it isn't very fun.
But mother says that I can't play
until my homework's done.

I wish that I could teach my dog
to do it all for me.
Then he could write a book report
while I climb up a tree.

TALLER

I think I'm growing taller,
a bit more every day,
but where my top will stop
I cannot estimate.

Every day I'm stretching
to make a taller me.
Perhaps I'll be a giant,
I'll just have to wait and see.

BATS

Bats are flying mammals
that steer themselves by sound.
They're small, furry creatures,
their ear size quite astounds.

They use their rubbery wings
to fly around at night,
zooming through the darkness
until the morning light.

Bats can live in caverns,
under bridges, or in trees.
They do their sleeping upside down
while hanging by their feet.

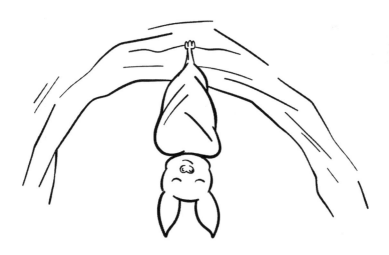

SEA SOUP

If the sea were made of soup
what flavor would it be?
Matzah Ball or Ramen?
Gazpacho or Split Pea?

Alphabet, or Miso,
Gumbo, Lentil, Leek?
If the sea were made of soup,
a giant spoon I'd seek.

AMADEUS OCTOPUS

Amadeus Octopus
loved to play piano.
While his eight arms caressed the keys,
he also sang soprano.

People crammed the concert halls,
his music was so sweet.
And all he asked for in return
were crabs and fish to eat.

He played with all the passion
that his three hearts could give,
but quit one day in a fit of rage
after being called a squid.

GIRAFFE AND GERBIL

Giraffe and Gerbil were friends,
though they didn't see eye to eye.
Gerbil lived close to the earth,
Giraffe was nearer the sky.

Gerbil would use a long ladder,
each day, so they could meet.
He would ascend to his tall friend,
beginning at her feet.

OODLES OF POODLES

Oodles and oodles of poodles,
playing in the park.
Oodles and oodles of poodles,
they bark and bark and bark.

Oodles of prancing poodles,
racing everywhere.
Oodles of poodle owners,
chasing them here and there.

Poodles with varying haircuts.
Poodles, both tiny and tall.
Millions and billions of poodles,
and I can't find mine at all.

SOMETHING FISHY

There's a catfish in the doghouse
and a tuna in the tub.
There's a goldfish in my soup dish
and a minnow in my mug.

There's a swordfish in the kitchen
chopping carrots into bits,
while a porpoise plays piano
in a suit that doesn't fit.

There's a marlin and monkfish
playing with a manta ray,
and a clownfish doing card tricks
while some sharks sip lemonade.

There's a flathead and a flounder
flopping on my parents' bed,
while a piranha and a pigfish
play inside the garden shed.

There's a bluegill blowing bubbles
and a salmon singing songs.
There's a sardine in my sneaker,
something fishy's going on!

GOODBYE SNOWMAN

My snowman's getting slimmer,
he's shrinking day by day.
His carrot nose has fallen,
now on the ground it lays.

The weather's not so frosty,
the sun is stronger now.
I fear that soon he'll turn into
a puddle on the ground.

ME, MYSELF, AND ODD

I'm really rather odd,
some might think me strange.
I'm just a little different,
but I know that's okay.

The world would be so boring
if we were all the same.
I'm glad to be uniquely me
and live life my own way.

HAROLD HOWARD HUNTER

Harold Howard Hunter
lives high atop a tree.
He loves to chirp with all the birds
and does so merrily.

A treehouse is his dwelling,
built when he was a child.
He moved in at the age of ten
and now he's sixty-five.

U.F.O.

I met a small, green spaceman
who landed in our yard.
His silver flying saucer
came crashing down quite hard.

He dented up his spaceship
and set the lawn aflame,
then seemed a wee bit cranky
when Father dared complain.

Mother made some lemonade
and said, "Here, rest a while."
And soon, the little astronaut
sat sipping with a smile.

His skin began to shimmer,
it glowed with greenish light,
and his long blue antennae
were wiggling with delight.

We thought that he said, "Thank you."
At least, that's how it seemed.
When he spoke, all we heard
were whistles, bloops, and beeps.

We longed to hear his stories
of far-off galaxies.
Wishing so, that we could know
the wonders that he's seen.

His ship had cooled off as he sat,
gone was the smoke and steam.
The green man opened up the hood
of his poor space machine.

He muttered as he fiddled
with gears and glowing wires.
He finished up and slammed it shut,
then quickly climbed inside.

He sat within the glassy dome
atop his silvery craft,
and all he left when flying off
were scorch marks on the grass.

Father grumbled, Mother waved,
while I stared up and grinned.
Each day I watch the skies to see
if he'll come back again.

PIZZA

Pizza, pizza, yes, let's eat,
for my taste buds, such a treat.

Pizza, pizza, grab a slice,
dipped in ranch sauce, oh so nice.

Pizza, pizza, melted cheese,
stretching out like gooey strings.

Pizza, pizza, oh yes please,
I think I'll seize just one more piece.

ICE CREAM IN SUMMER

Eating ice cream in summer
is a race against time.
Everything's melting,
it's scorching outside.

I am eating this ice cream
just as fast as I can.
It runs down the cone,
then drips on my hand.

The cone's getting soggy,
I have a brain freeze.
Don't plop on the ground,
I'm begging you, please!

MOOSE ON THE LOOSE

There's a moose on the loose
and it's running through our town.
There's some grouse in the house
flinging feathers all around.

There's a bear in my chair
eating honey with a spoon.
There's a pig in a wig
dancing with a big raccoon.

There's a crow with a bow
shooting arrows at the sun.
There's a shark in the park
playing tennis just for fun.

There's a stork with a fork
dining on some fish and chips.
There's a goat skipping rope
while a hippo does backflips.

All these things must be dreams,
they're too silly to be true.
But I really must wake up
before another moose gets loose.

ADVENTURES IN EGYPT

I'd like to climb the pyramid
at Giza, near the Nile,
or sit beside the silent Sphinx
to simply think a while.

I'd talk with Tutankhamun
if he was still alive,
watch Cleopatra paint her eyes
with kohl and malachite.

I'd sleep in a sarcophagus,
wrapped in my mummy suit,
and to startle archeologists,
I'd jump up and shout "BOO!"

WHOOO?

"Who's there?"
the gray owl hoots,
"Who, who, who?"
As it sails in the silver light
of the moon, moon, moon.

"Just we,"
the crickets answer,
"Creak, creak, creak,"
as a field mouse sleeps
in its burrow beneath
the old oak tree.

FOZZLE-WOZZLE

The dreadful Fozzle-Wozzle
is a very fearsome foe.
It sneezes out hot fireballs
everywhere it goes.

Crying tears of lava
and coughing stinky smoke.
Its awful rotten-egg stench
will make you start to choke.

You'll need a giant squirt gun
or a long green garden hose,
to stop the Fozzle-Wozzle
and its raging, blazing nose.

SOMEONE TOOK THE COOKIES

Someone took the cookies.
Oh, what have they done?
Someone took the cookies,
now all that's left is crumbs.
Someone took the cookies,
a thief is in this house.
Someone took the cookies...
it must have been a mouse!

BELCHING BENNY

Benny the belching burro
burped an awful lot
whenever he ate asparagus,
apples, or apricots.

We tried to teach him manners,
but Benny refused to learn.
"I need to let my burps out,
or else my tummy burns."

Benny was terribly gassy,
his case seemed quite severe.
We brought him to a doctor
who checked his throat and ears.

"I think I see the problem,"
the kindly doctor said.
"His brain's down in his tummy
and there's nothing in his head.

When the Doc put Benny's brain back
in the place where it belonged,
his tummy had room for food,
all the gassiness was gone.

Then everyone celebrated,
the party was lively and loud.
And Benny seemed very content
to eat without making a sound.

SLEEPYHEAD

Oh no, oh no,
I've overslept!
The day has run away.
Everyone else is already up
while I'm so very late.

Oh no, oh no,
I've overslept!
I'm such a sleepyhead.
The only sensible thing to do
is just go back to bed.

SHOO FLU

I think I caught a cold,
or perhaps a cold caught me.
My eyes are red and droopy.
My nose just wants to sneeze.

I'm told I have a fever of
one hundred and one degrees.
My throat's so sore and swollen.
Shoo flu, it's time to leave.

THE ANTEATER'S NOSE

I thought anteaters
ate food with their nose.
Where did I learn that?
Cartoons, I suppose.

An anteater's nose
knows what it loves to eat.
Termites and ants are
its favorite treat.

No teeth in its mouth,
a long, sticky tongue.
Sniffing, then slurping,
it eats on the run.

An anteater's life
would never suit me.
The food on their menu
would bug me, you see.

GRANDPA'S IN THE TREE AGAIN

Grandpa's in the tree again,
he's hanging upside down.
Grandpa's in the tree again,
his teeth have fallen out.

Grandpa's in the tree again,
we're worried that he'll slip.
Grandpa's in the tree again,
but he's not scared one bit.

Grandpa's having too much fun,
he won't cooperate.
Someone bring a safety net
before it is too late.

MY KITE

The wind sends my kite
soaring up in the sky,
swooping and swaying,
as if it's come alive.

My kite does a dance,
as it yearns to be free.
Our only connection,
this long, slender string.

But if I should let go,
it would come crashing down.
For my kite to fly high,
it needs me on the ground.

STRANGE WEATHER

It's raining cats and dogs,
and hailing javelinas.
It's snowing snails and frogs,
there's a hurricane of hyenas.

The day is cold and gray,
though the sun is burning bright.
I can't go out and play,
a toad-nato's roaring by!

SILLY HAIR

The land of dreams
is a magical place,
but in the morning
when I see my face,
I sometimes wonder
what happened there,
to make me wake up
with this wild, wacky hair.

KYLE CRISPIN CROCODILE

Kyle Crispin Crocodile
has a mighty frightening mouth.
His teeth are tough and terrible
inside his scaly snout.

Kyle is strong and fearless,
his bite is quite a menace.
The only thing Kyle Crispin dreads
is going to the dentist.

RAINY DAY

It's raining hard
this gloomy day,
I wish the rain
would go away.

The lightning's flash
and thunder's boom
makes me so glad
I'm in my room.

When this storm's end
brings sunny skies,
a sparkling world
will await outside.

ANTHONY PLAID

Anthony Plaid
was a handsome young lad
with a nose adored by the sun.

It burned and turned red
though he covered his head
so straight to the shade, he'd run.

In five minutes at most,
it looked like burned toast
slathered with strawberry jam.

But his nose is now safe
in a fine woolen cape
knitted for him by his loving Gran.

THE FICKLE FELINE

This cat will let you stroke its fur,
this cat will arch its back and purr.
But when it's had enough of nice—
this cat might scratch,
this cat might bite.

CINNAMON TOAST

Cinnamon toast, cinnamon toast,
the kind of toast I love the most.
I don't want to brag,
I don't want to boast,
but I like toast with cinnamon.

Cinnamon toast, cinnamon toast,
three slices at a minimum—
I don't want to brag,
I don't want to boast,
but I like toast with cinnamon.

TAILSPIN

Sometimes my dog
chases her tail,
around and around again.
She strives so hard
to catch herself,
she tries nine times, then ten.

My dizzy dog
has so much fun,
as she, in circles, spins.
She turns so fast
it's hard to tell
her beginning from her end.

GRAMPA'S HAIRS

Grandpa has eyebrows
so bushy and fierce.
Grandpa has hairs
growing out of his ears!

On the backs of his hands
and the tops of his toes...
He even has hairs
growing out of his nose!

I can't help but wonder
when I'm very old,
will my wandering hairs
be so gray and so bold?

OWWW!

Tiny toe, BIG PAIN.
Lightning flash in my brain.
I stub it, then I rub it,
to take the ache away.
Why do my toes so often find
hard things on which to bang?

WHO MADE THIS MESS?

Who threw my clothes down on the floor?
It wasn't me, of that, I'm sure!

These dirty clothes, they make a mess,
a stranger left them there, I guess.

It's hard to walk, they're everywhere!
They'll trip you up, so please beware.

Just how they got there, no one knows...
I guess I should pick up my clothes.

PIRATE PEG

Pirate Peg was a fearsome foe
who sailed the Seven Seas.
She had a parrot named Terrible Tess
who loudly squawked and sneezed.

Peg was named for her missing leg,
blown off by a cannon ball.
The leg was replaced by a wooden stake
which helped her stand up tall.

Peg flew a flag of skull and bones,
and plundered, as pirates do.
She buried her loot on desert isles
and hid the maps in her old leather boot.

THIS FLY

This fly must be
in love with me.
It's the only reason
I can see
for why this fly
would choose my face,
of all the people
in this place.

My face, my face,
its landing space,
fly feet tickling
on my face.
Though I shoo it
with my hands,
the fly zooms by me
once again.

See, oh see!
Look, there it goes.
It tried to fly
right up my nose.
This fly's in love,
but I am not.
Please go away
or SWAT! SWAT! SWAT!

HOW TO TAME A DRAGON

Someone let the dragon loose,
it's roaming free again.
They left the cage door open
now it will not go back in.

It's setting fire to houses
with flaming dragon breath.
Frightening all the people
and making quite a mess.

I think I might know how to calm
that fearsome creature down,
a way to stop the dragon
from burning up our town.

It surely must be lonely,
it's the only one around.
Perhaps it's longing for the place
where dragons still abound.

If someone would just listen,
I can explain my plan.
I'll tame the dragon with tall tales
of life in fairy land.

I don't know how it got here,
so very far from home.
I'll read the dragon stories
then it won't feel so alone.

STORY TIME

My mother reads me stories,
she reads them oh, so well.
She makes up different voices
for every tale she tells.

She might sound like a pirate,
a dragon, or a queen,
a very scary giant
or a boy with magic beans.

She reads them like a movie
that I see in my head,
and though it's almost bedtime,
"Just one more page," I beg.

GOODNIGHT

Close your eyes
you sleepyhead.
Close your eyes
it's time for bed.

Rest your body,
rest your mind.
Dream sweet dreams
till morning time.

Goodbye for now. I hope you'll
visit these poems again soon.

ABOUT THE AUTHOR

JOHN MARK GREEN

My earliest poetry memories are of my mother reading aloud from a little book called Silver Pennies. Her dramatic readings of poems and stories captured my imagination, and when I had children of my own, I loved reading to them.

I was born in Kentucky but have lived in Arizona most of my life. I love cinnamon toast, and tacos are my favorite food. I've never met a woolly mammoth, but I hope to one day.

I'm the author of the poetry book Taste the Wild Wonder and am married to the wonderful Canadian poet Christy Ann Martine. I Met a Woolly Mammoth is my first book for children.

ABOUT THE ILLUSTRATOR

AYA SUARJAYA

I am a cartoon artist from Bali, Indonesia. I have never studied at art school, but I've enjoyed drawing since I was little because I love watching cartoons and anime. I also love robots, action figures, and toys. When I was a kid, I loved drawing anime characters, comics, and all my favorite things. My study books were full of drawings.

Made in the USA
Middletown, DE
22 October 2022

13288532R00050